Exploring Ancient

EGYPT

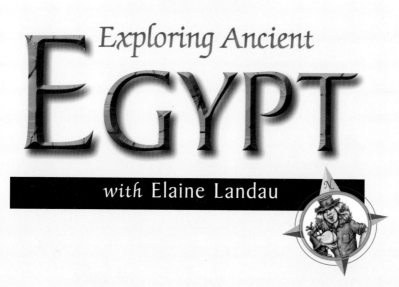

with Elaine Landau

Enslow Elementary

an imprint of

Enslow Publishers, Inc.

40 Industrial Road   PO Box 38
Box 398   Aldershot
Berkeley Heights, NJ 07922   Hants GU12 6BP
USA   UK

http://www.enslow.com

"The 'Exploring Ancient Civilizations With Elaine Landau' series tells the stories of the Egyptians, Greeks, Romans, Chinese, Vikings, and Aztecs with texts and illustrations designed to appeal to a broad spectrum of students. While not refraining from acknowledging injustice, hardship, and even the brutality of pre-modern civilizations, the series nonetheless succeeds in presenting these six ancient peoples in a dignified, praiseworthy, and even exemplary light. Highly recommended."

—Nicholas F. Jones, Professor of Classics, University of Pittsburgh

For Shari A. Witkoff, a terrific dentist and person

Enslow Elementary, an imprint of Enslow Publishers, Inc.

Enslow Elementary ® is a registered trademark of Enslow Publishers, Inc.

Library of Congress Cataloging-in-Publication Data

Landau, Elaine.
    Exploring ancient Egypt with Elaine Landau / Elaine Landau.— 1st ed.
      p. cm. — (Exploring ancient civilizations with Elaine Landau)
    Includes bibliographical references and index.
    ISBN 0-7660-2339-7
    1. Egypt—Civilization—To 332 B.C.—Juvenile literature. 2. Egypt—Civilization—
332 B.C.-638 A.D.—Juvenile literature. I. Title. II. Series.
    DT61.L32 2005
    932—dc22
                        2004016151

Printed in the United States of America

10 9 8 7 6 5 4 3 2 1

To Our Readers: We have done our best to make sure all Internet addresses in this book were active and appropriate when we went to press. However, the author and the publisher have no control over and assume no liability for the material available on those Internet sites or on other Web sites they may link to. Any comments or suggestions can be sent by e-mail to comments@enslow.com or to the address on the back cover.

Illustration Credits: Clipart.com, pp. 21 (bottom), 36 (bottom), 38 (top); © Corel Corporation, pp. 1, 2, 5 (insets), 7 (top), 8 (bottom), 11, 12, 13, 14, 15, 16, 17 (top), 18, 20, 21 (top), 22, 23 (bottom), 24 (top), 26 (bottom), 27, 28 (background), 29 (top), 31, 33 (top), 34 (bottom), 35 (top and bottom left), 40, 41 (top), 45; Dave Pavelonis, pp. 3, 7 (bottom), 9 (bottom), 10, 17 (bottom), 19 (top), 24 (bottom), 29 (bottom), 30, 35 (bottom right), 37 (top), 38 (bottom), 41 (bottom) and Compasses on pp. 1, 5, 6, 42; Dover Publications, Inc., p. 46; Elaine Landau, p. 42; Enslow Publishers, Inc., pp. 4–5, 25, 28; Gian Luigi Scarfiotti/Saudi Aramco World/PADIA, p. 33 (bottom); John Feeney/Saudi Aramco World/PADIA, pp. 9 (top), 36 (top), 37 (bottom); Kristin McCarthy, p. 19 (bottom); Photos.com, pp. 6, 8 (top), 23 (top), 26 (top), 28 (background), 32, 34 (top), 39, 40, 44.

Front Cover Illustration: Dave Pavelonis (Compass); © Corel Corporation (All Egypt photos)

Back Cover Illustration: Dave Pavelonis (Compass); © Corel Corporation (Queen Nefertiti)

Contents

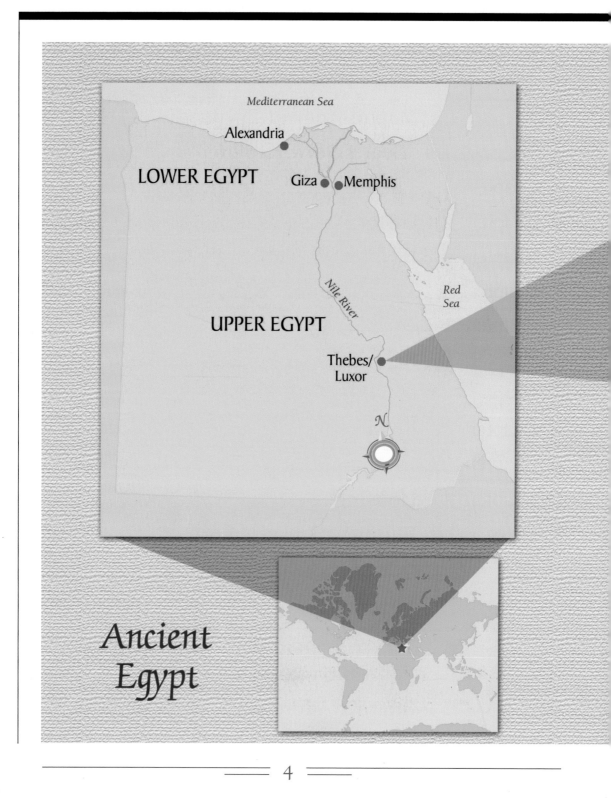

Mediterranean Sea

Alexandria

LOWER EGYPT

Giza ● ●Memphis

Nile River

UPPER EGYPT

Red Sea

Thebes/
Luxor ●

N

*Ancient
Egypt*

Valley of the Kings

■ Temple of Hatshepsut

Valley of
the Queens

■ Temple of
Ramses II

■ Karnak Temple

THEBES

Dear Fellow Explorer,

What if you could travel back in time? If you could go anywhere in the world, where would it be? Would visiting an ancient civilization interest you? The country I have in mind has huge pyramids, magnificent temples, and towering monuments. While there, you could see hieroglyphic writing or look at a 365-day calendar created thousands of years ago. Before leaving, you might want to learn how mummies are prepared for burial.

If you think this sounds like an exciting trip, get ready to go. You will be traveling thousands of years back in time. Head for the banks of the Nile River in Northeast Africa. You will be on your way to ancient Egypt.

I'm Elaine Landau and this is my dog Max. Max and I are about to visit ancient Egypt. The trip

Ancient Egypt's pyramids rise high above the sands below.

This hieroglyphic writing includes pictures of a bird, a fish, and musical instruments.

was Max's idea. He loves time traveling and wanted to see the pyramids. Come along with us. There is a lot to see. No need to worry about the time—with time travel you can always be back before dinner. To start your journey, just turn the page!

The Importance of the Nile

*A*ncient Egypt was sometimes called "the gift of the Nile." The Nile River flowed through six hundred miles of it and emptied into the Mediterranean Sea. That was about the length of the entire country. As its "gift," the Nile brought rich soil to the desert.

Every summer the Nile flooded over its banks. The flood left a thick layer of rich dark mud on the land. This made the dry desert soil fertile.

A crocodile suns itself in the waters of the Nile River.

The Egyptians dug irrigation canals that delivered water from the Nile to dry land.

This reed boat is being made using the same process as the ancient Egyptians.

Since the soil was fertile, the ancient Egyptians could grow crops and plant fig trees and date palms. Cattle could graze on the grassy green areas. Having fertile land allowed ancient Egypt to feed its people. It used these crops in trading with other nations as well.

The river was important in other ways too. It was a major means for transporting both grain and stone used for building. To do this, the ancient Egyptians built long boats made of tightly bound reeds from the Nile. The Nile River was ancient Egypt's lifeline. Without it, the country would have been just another stretch of desert.

LET'S STOP HERE. I FEEL LIKE SNACKING ON SOME TASTY FIGS AND DATES!

The earliest Egyptians wandered, tending herds of animals. They traveled from place to place. Then, about seven thousand years ago, these groups began to settle. They formed small farming villages. Soon there were a number of these villages in two regions known as Lower Egypt and Upper Egypt.

According to legend, around 3100 B.C., an Upper Egyptian King named Menes conquered Lower Egypt. He joined the two regions to form one nation. The country of Egypt was born.

Menes started the first Egyptian dynasty. A dynasty is a group of rulers from the same family. Usually a dynasty will rule over a long period. In most cases, the right to rule passes from father to son. Through the centuries, thirty dynasties ruled Egypt.

The rulers were extremely powerful. Egyptians did not think of them as mere men. They thought of their rulers as gods in human form.

WHEN THERE WERE NO SONS IN THE ROYAL FAMILY TO RULE . . . THEN A DAUGHTER MIGHT TAKE THE THRONE.

I THINK THEY SHOULD HAVE GIVEN A DOG A SHOT AT THE JOB!

Much of ancient Egyptian history is usually divided into three periods known as the Old, Middle, and New Kingdoms. The first period, the Old Kingdom, lasted from about 2686 B.C. to 2181 B.C. During this time, Egypt's great pyramids were built. In the years following the Old

The great pyramids in Giza were built during the time of the Old Kingdom.

Kingdom, not a lot happened in Egypt. The rulers during this time were not particularly outstanding.

Things improved during the Middle Kingdom period from about 2055 B.C. to 1650 B.C. Trade with other nations increased. The arts and architecture got better, too. Following the end of this period, a number of weak kings ruled. They were no match for the invaders from Asia who seized control of Egypt for about one hundred years. These foreign rulers were known as the Hyksos kings.

Egypt's glory would again shine during the New Kingdom period from about 1550 B.C. to 1295 B.C. At this point in their history, Egyptians began calling their rulers pharaohs. Under the pharaohs of this period, the nation reached new heights. It developed a strong army and conquered other countries. These became part of Egypt's expanding empire. In time, Egypt grew to be one of the most powerful and wealthy nations in the ancient world.

Some of the outstanding pharaohs of this period are still studied today. One famous female ruler was Queen Hatshepsut—the wife of a pharaoh who died in about 1490 B.C. Hatshepsut's stepson was supposed to become pharaoh but he was still too young. So Hatshepsut took

Mortuary Temple was built into the side of a cliff for Queen Hatshepsut. When the temple was first built, a path of trees and statues led up to it.

over as queen and when her stepson grew older, she ruled alongside him. Hatshepsut is famous for fearlessly leading soldiers into battle to extend Egypt's empire. She also increased trade with other nations.

Another well-known Egyptian ruler was King Tutankhamun. He reigned from about 1347 B.C. to 1339 B.C. Tutankhamun is sometimes called the boy king because he became pharaoh when he was just nine years old and died at the age of eighteen. Tutankhamun became

The mask of King Tut is made mostly of gold and was found covering the head and shoulders of the king's mummy.

known throughout the world in 1922 when Howard Carter discovered his tomb nearly undisturbed. In it were over five thousand riches and treasures. These included bows and arrows, chariots, necklaces, bracelets, daggers, toys, and games.

Still another famous pharaoh from the New Kingdom period was Ramses II. The reign of Ramses II lasted from about 1290 B.C. to 1224 B.C. During that time, he built many magnificent temples and monuments throughout ancient Egypt.

At the Great Temple of Ramses II, many large statues of the pharaoh can be seen. The likenesses of Ramses II are so big that each mouth is three feet wide! Over time, the statues have lost the many colors they once had.

Yet, this fruitful time did not last. Following the New Kingdom period, the country was invaded by a number of foreign forces. In 332 B.C., the Macedonian conqueror Alexander the Great took over Egypt. Macedonia was a country to the north of Greece, but Alexander the Great also ruled Greece itself.

In 323 B.C., Alexander the Great died of a fever. One of his generals, Ptolemy, became king of Egypt. Ptolemy began his own dynasty—these rulers were known as the

Ptolemies. The Ptolemies brought Greek art and culture to Egypt. They built wonderful libraries and museums. They also constructed shrines and temples to Egyptian gods. The Ptolemies enriched Egypt by increasing foreign trade as well.

Queen Cleopatra VII was the daughter of Ptolemy XIII. Cleopatra and her ten-year-old brother took the throne of Egypt in 51 B.C. following their father's death. Cleopatra is often portrayed as a great beauty in films. However, there is no evidence as to how the real Cleopatra looked. Instead, she was known for her intelligence and wit. She was also said to be extremely ambitious and cunning.

In 30 B.C., ancient Egypt fell to Rome. Cleopatra committed suicide by allowing herself to be bitten by a poisonous snake. Egypt became part of the Roman Empire. Today, Egypt is once again an independent nation and the memory of ancient Egypt's splendor lives on.

The head of Cleopatra is etched in stone. On each side is a deadly cobra.

3 Egyptian Society

Egyptian society was made up of different classes. At the highest level were the pharaoh and royal family. Below them was an upper class of priests, wealthy landowners, and those in high public office. Ancient Egypt's middle class included highly skilled craftsmen and professionals in the arts and sciences.

Most Egyptians, however, were part of the lower class. These were the common laborers. These Egyptians did the farming, bending, lifting, and carrying that was needed.

Slaves were at the bottom of society. Most were captives from wars. Slaves worked as servants and laborers. They could be sold by their owners at any time.

People could move up or down in class. Sometimes

Pharaohs had pyramids built over their tombs. This step pyramid was one of the first pyramids built by the Egyptians.

This painting shows goldsmiths at work (top). In the middle, men make pottery. At the bottom, workers are making bricks.

this was done through marriage. Other times it was the result of doing a job well. Even slaves could be freed and work their way up from the lower class of Egyptian society.

Family life was important. The father was the head of the family. The women still had many rights, however. They could own property. They had the right to divorce their husbands as well.

Most ancient Egyptian women took care of their children, cooked, cleaned, wove cloth, and sewed. They taught their daughters to do the same. Some women from poor families worked alongside their husbands in the fields.

Most boys learned to do the same work their fathers did. Few children went to school. However, some boys from upper-class families studied reading, writing, geography, and math.

WOULD I HAVE HAD A PLACE IN ANCIENT EGYPTIAN SOCIETY?

OF COURSE YOU WOULD MAX. MANY EGYPTIAN CHILDREN HAD PETS...CATS, MONKEYS, AND OF COURSE DOGS!

The World of Work

Many different types of workers made ancient Egypt a success. The largest number of workers farmed the land. Most worked on estates owned by wealthy families. Wheat, barley, lettuce, beans, onions, dates, grapes, melons, and other foods were grown there. Not all estates produced food crops. A plant called flax was grown as well. It was used to make fine Egyptian linen. The ancient Egyptians also used the oil from its seeds.

A good deal of mining was done in ancient Egypt. It was a land rich in minerals. Workers took tin, gold, and copper out of the ground. They cut away limestone,

Most of the ancient Egyptians tended the Nile Valley's fertile farmland.

THEY DUG CANALS TO CARRY WATER FROM THE NILE TO THE FIELDS. THE PROCESS IS CALLED **IRRIGATION!**

HOW DO YOU SUPPOSE THEY GREW ALL THESE CROPS IN THIS **HOT DRY CLIMATE?**

sandstone, and granite too. These were used to construct the monuments, buildings, sculptures, and beautiful stone vases.

There were no large factories in ancient Egypt. Craftsmen in their shops made much of what people needed. Carpenters produced furniture, statues, game boards, and coffins. Artisans or jewelry makers made beautiful gold and copper necklaces, bracelets, pins, and earrings.

Potters made water jugs and cooking pots. Metalsmiths made tools and weapons. Still other craftsmen used plant fibers to make rope and weave baskets. The ancient Egyptians also made a type of paper from the papyrus plant.

Some ancient Egyptians were merchant traders who sailed to

Papyrus paper is thought to have first been used in 4000 B.C. The Egyptians kept the technique for making it secret. The papyrus at the right was made by using ancient methods.

distant lands. There they traded Egyptian goods for products needed back home. They brought back spices, silver, iron, horses, special types of cattle, and other items.

There were other groups of workers in ancient Egypt as well. Among these were professionals who provided services in different areas. This group included architects, engineers, scientists, musicians, artists, and others.

Medicine was quite advanced in ancient Egypt and doctors were highly thought of. These doctors knew how to clean and treat cuts and wounds as well as set broken bones so that they healed properly. They also developed various potions or medicines to cure certain illnesses.

The two workers in this temple mural are sanding a table.

Some Egyptians hunted animals for food.

Scribes were very important as well. They often knew several forms of writing. This helped them write letters for the pharaoh and keep track of everything that happened in ancient Egypt. Good record keeping was important to the smooth running of the country.

Though the ancient Egyptians worked hard, they did not earn any money. Money was not used in ancient Egypt. People were paid for their work in goods or services. When they wanted to buy something, they paid for it with the goods or services they produced.

Scribes recorded the history of ancient Egypt. They also wrote on scrolls of a special kind of paper called papyrus.

Architecture

Ancient Egypt is famous for its architecture, which is the design of buildings. Large and splendid palaces and temples were built there. Many of these had tall columns shaped like palm trees or other plants. These buildings also had numerous rooms and open courtyards.

The ancient Egyptians also constructed many different monuments for their pharaohs and gods. Among the most impressive were the pyramids. Pyramids were huge structures in which pharaohs were buried. The sides of a pyramid were shaped like triangles. On later pyramids these sides met at a point at the top. Earlier pyramids had flat tops. Some pyramids were made of stone while others were made of dried mud bricks. Still other pyramids were just

The Kiosk of Trajan is made up mostly of fancy columns. It was built after the Romans took over ancient Egypt.

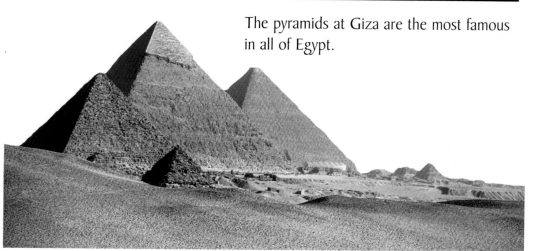

The pyramids at Giza are the most famous in all of Egypt.

rubble held in place by an outer stone casing.

The interior or inside of the pyramids varied as well. Some were built with many different chambers. Other Egyptian pyramids were simply hollow inside. They were built over the top of burial chambers in the ground.

Yet because of its size, building any pyramid took

The ancient Egyptians built obelisks. These structures were square columns that ended with a point at the top.

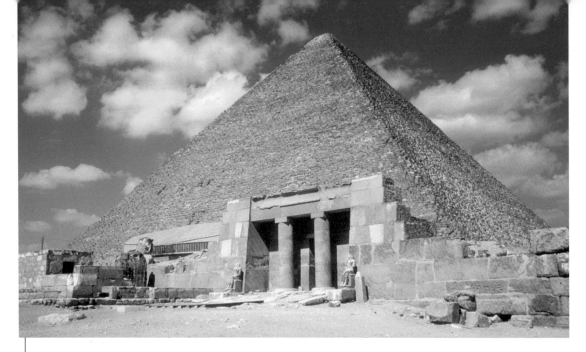

The Great Pyramid was ordered to be built by King Khufu. Its entrance was used by the Egyptian builders who worked on the inside.

I WOULD HATE TO TUMBLE DOWN FROM **THE TOP!**

I KNOW, MAX! WHILE BUILDING THE PYRAMIDS, MANY WORKERS FELL TO THEIR **DEATHS.**

a great deal of time, effort, and planning. Thousands of individuals had to work from twenty to thirty years just to finish one. Many people mistakenly think that slaves built ancient Egypt's pyramids. However, skeletons along with other remains help prove that the pyramid builders were actually Egyptian laborers. These workers lived in special villages near the building sites. Work on

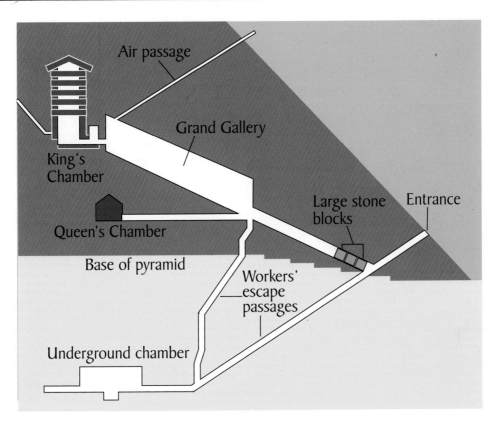

When the workers were done building the Great Pyramid, they released large stone blocks that closed off the passage to the king's chamber. They then left through escape passages.

the pyramids was overseen by foremen or supervisors appointed by the pharaoh.

The Great Pyramid at Giza is Egypt's largest pyramid. Today it stands 454 feet tall and contains 2 million limestone blocks. The Great Pyramid is considered one of the Seven Wonders of the Ancient World. Ancient travelers wanted to see it on their journeys. Travelers to Egypt today still visit its ruins.

6 Religion

*T*he ancient Egyptians believed in many gods and goddesses. One of their most important gods was called Ra. He was the sun god. Living in a hot desert climate, the sun was central to Egyptian life. It is not surprising that Ra was so honored.

Isis was the main Egyptian goddess. She represented the loyal and caring wife and mother. Isis's husband was also her brother. He was a god named Osiris. Osiris was known as the god of vegetation (plant

This statue of the god Anubis shows him with the head of a jackal. The god Ra was shown in many different forms: a cat, a bird, a lion, or the sun itself.

The goddess Isis extends her winged arms in this tomb painting.

The goddess Hathor sits and awaits gifts from Cleopatra, an Egyptian queen. Hathor was the goddess of love, music, and women.

growth) as well as the god of the dead. Isis and Osiris had a son called Horus. Horus was a god of the sky. He has been drawn as having a human body and a falcon's head. Egyptian rulers were believed to be a form of Horus living on Earth.

The ancient Egyptians also worshiped many lesser gods. People living in different towns and cities had their own special

Tourists love to visit Karnak Temple because it has so many statues. Out in front of the temple is the statue of Pharaoh Pinodjem.

Egyptian Gods and Goddesses

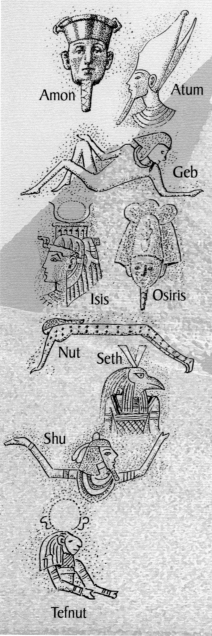

Amon

Atum

Geb

Isis

Osiris

Nut Seth

Shu

Tefnut

There were dozens of gods and goddesses that the ancient Egyptians worshipped. Below are some of the most important.

Amon—King of the Gods to those who lived in and around Thebes.

Anubis—God of mummification.

Atum—God of the setting sun.

Geb—God of the earth.

Hathor—Goddess of love, music, and women.

Horus—God of the sun and the pharaohs.

Isis—Goddess of magic.

Nut—Goddess of the sky.

Osiris—God of the afterlife.

Ra—Creator god of the sun.

Seth—God of storms and chaos.

Shu—God of the air.

Tefnut—Goddess of moisture and rain.

Thoth—God of wisdom and the moon.

Karnak Temple was probably the largest temple complex built. It consisted of three main temples: two for the gods Amon and Montu, and one for the goddess Mut.

gods. The same was true for people in different professions.

The Egyptians did not pray at their temples. The magnificent temples were used for other purposes. Some temples were the homes of different gods and goddesses. Others were built to receive offerings (gifts) for an Egyptian ruler who had died. These were often attached to the pharaoh's pyramid or tomb. Priests were the loyal keepers of these temples. They prayed to the gods and performed other religious rites. This included putting out food and offerings for them.

SOME ANCIENT EGYPTIANS WORSHIPPED THE CAT GODDESS BASTET. WHY NOT WORSHIP A WONDERFUL DOG LIKE ME?

7 Afterlife

*T*he ancient Egyptians did not believe that life ended at death. They thought that there was an afterlife—or a life after death. The ancient Egyptians felt that it was possible for people to be renewed at death and go on to enjoy everlasting life. In this eternal life, they would never grow old or be sick. They would also not be troubled by things that might have worried them in their earlier life.

DID YOU KNOW THAT SOME ANCIENT EGYPTIANS **MUMMIFIED THEIR PETS** WHEN THEY DIED?

MAX

The ancient Egyptians believed they would need their bodies in the next life. So they tried to stop them from decaying. To do this, they mummified or preserved the dead. Nearly all Egyptians who could afford it arranged to become mummies when they died. Over a period spanning about three thousand years, it is believed that about 70 million mummies were created.

Mummifying a dead body involved a number of steps.

Many of the body's organs were stored in special jars called canopic jars. These jars often had human or animal heads carved at the top.

First, the person's lungs, liver, stomach, intestines, and brain were removed. The brain was thrown away. The other organs were dried and stored in special jars. Then the body was covered with a type of salt to dry it out. This helped to prevent decay. Later the body was tightly wrapped in many yards of linen. Each finger and toe was separately wrapped. Sometimes a mummy mask was also placed over the face.

This tomb painting shows the Egyptian god Anubis. He is making a dead man into a mummy.

At that point, the mummy was put in a coffin or mummy case. Coffins in ancient Egypt were made of stone, wood, or layers of linen and plaster. These cases were painted with colorful scenes and religious symbols. They were believed to magically protect the person. The earliest mummy cases were just rectangular boxes. Later on, they were shaped like the human body.

After prayers were said, the mummy was put in a tomb. Clothes, food, jewelry, and other items were placed in the tomb as well. The ancient Egyptians thought that a dead person would need these in the next life. Small statues of workers and servants were also put in the tombs of the rich. These were to do manual labor and farming for the person in the afterlife.

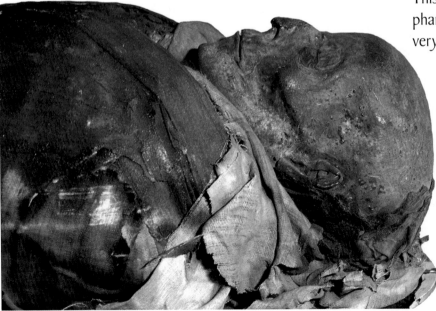

This mummy of the pharoah Ramses II is very well-preserved.

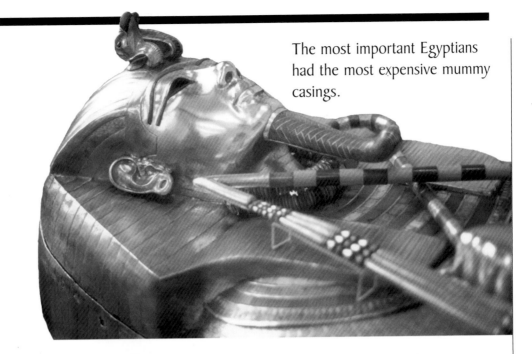

The most important Egyptians had the most expensive mummy casings.

The ancient Egyptians had pictures of everyday activities painted on the tomb walls. They had special prayers or spells written on the walls too. These prayers were supposed to guide and protect the person in the afterlife. They came from a special book called the Book of the Dead. Sometimes a copy of this book might be put in the tomb as well.

In the center is a statue of the cat goddess Bastet. On the left and right are mummified cats.

Food

Wheat and barley were the two main crops of ancient Egypt. This could be seen in people's daily diets. The ancient Egyptians made bread out of wheat and beer out of barley. Vegetables and fruits were also commonly eaten in ancient Egypt. Sometimes grapes were used to make wine or raisins.

Wheat and barley were planted in the fertile soil near the Nile River.

Upper-class ancient Egyptians had a fair amount of meat in their diets. They ate antelope, oxen, sheep, pigs, and goats. They also liked poultry and often ate geese and ducks. Some of these birds were wild. Others were raised to be eaten.

These two Egyptian geese would have made a nice meal for a hungry upper-class Egyptian family.

All types of food were shared by Egyptians at temple festivals.

Most poor Egyptians could not afford meat. They only ate it once in a while during temple festivals. Usually fish from the Nile River was an important part of their diet.

Wealthy Egyptians were known to like fancy cakes. Expert bakers made these for the rich. The cakes were sweetened with figs. Sometimes bakers also used honey. They got honey from beekeepers in the area who raised bees in order to harvest the honey.

Dates were a popular food in ancient Egypt.

THIS SURE BEATS **DOG FOOD!**

Clothing

The ancient Egyptians never needed coats or boots. Living in a hot climate, they kept their clothing light. Most of their clothes were linen, a cloth made from the flax plant.

White dresses kept women cooler in the summer.

Women usually wore long white linen dresses. The men wore linen skirts wrapped around the waist and tied in a knot. At times, both men and women wore cloaks or robes as well. Both also wore simple sandals made of leather or from reeds of the papyrus plant taken from the Nile River.

Beauty was important in ancient Egypt. Both women and men tried to look their best. Wealthy Egyptians wore

This Egyptian sandal was made from the papyrus plant.

jewelry to add to their attractiveness. Fancy rings, bracelets, necklaces, and earrings were popular.

The ancient Egyptians used makeup and perfume too. Men and women outlined their eyes. They applied rouge to their cheeks and lips. Wigs were common as well. Many Egyptians had a good supply of grooming aids. They owned combs, makeup containers, hair-curling devices, mirrors, and razors for shaving.

The man on the left is dressed like an Egyptian noble.

Housing

There were different types of houses in ancient Egypt. Where you lived usually depended on who you were. No one knows for sure what the homes of poor laborers were like. But it is generally thought that these dwellings were not very big or fancy. They were probably little more than crude huts.

Most Egyptian homes were very simple.

AFTER SEEING THIS...
I COULD NEVER GO BACK TO A
DOG HOUSE!!

Middle-class Egyptian homes were much larger. Usually these had at least three rooms. Some of these homes were on one level. Others had two or three stories. Still, these houses could not compare with the homes of very wealthy Egyptians.

Much of Egypt's upper class lived in luxury. Some of their homes were quite large with over fifty rooms. These homes could have more than three floors. The

The lotus flower added some color to the garden pools of wealthy Egyptians. The lotus was very special to Egyptians. The flower even appeared in their artwork.

walls of the rooms were painted with brightly colored designs or nature scenes. This seemed to bring the outdoors inside.

These homes usually had beautiful gardens surrounding them. Some even had gardens of trees called orchards. Fig and date trees were very common. Often in the center of a garden was a large pool. It would be filled with floating lotus flowers and a variety of fish.

Yet in some ways, all ancient Egyptian homes were alike. Most had only small windows placed high up on the walls. This kept the inside of the house cool. Only a little heat and sunlight came through. These windows also caught the cool breeze from the north. Egyptians would soak mats in water and leave them on the floor.

This also helped cool their homes. On really hot nights, ancient Egyptians would sleep on their roofs!

Most ancient Egyptian homes were built with sun-dried bricks. The bricks were made of mud from the Nile River mixed with pieces of straw and small stones. The outside of the homes was usually covered with plaster. They used the trunks of palm trees to support the roofs of their houses.

Mud-brick homes overlook a river in Egypt today. These homes are much like those built by ancient Egyptians.

Exiting Ancient Egypt

11

Ancient Egypt was a fabulous place. Today there are countless reminders of its glory. Its temples, pyramids, and sculptures are just a few of the treasures of this ancient land. Egypt is a country with a proud past.

Going to ancient Egypt was great. But now Max and I must

Don't leave Egypt without seeing the Great Sphinx at Giza. It has the head of a man and the body of a lion and is more than forty-five hundred years old!

be heading home. We are delighted that you came with us. Exploring the past is always more fun with friends. To the time machine!

Farewell Fellow Explorer,

Just wanted to take a moment to tell you a little about the real "Max and me." I am a children's book author and Max is a small, fluffy, white dog. I almost named him Marshmallow because of how he looks. However, he seems to think he's human—so only a more dignified name would do. Max also seems to think that he is a large, powerful dog. He fearlessly chases after much larger dogs in the neighborhood. Max was thrilled when the artist for this book drew him as a dog several times his size. He felt that someone in the art world had finally captured his true spirit.

In real life, Max is quite a traveler. I've taken him to nearly every state while doing research for different books. We live in Florida, so when we go north, I have to pack a sweater for him. When we were in Oregon, it rained and I was glad I brought his raincoat. None of this gear is necessary when time traveling. My "take off" spot is the computer station and, as always, Max sits faithfully by my side.

Best Wishes,
Elaine & Max (a small dog with big dreams)

Timeline

4000 B.C.	Ancient Egyptians begin using hieroglyphic writing.
3100 B.C.	Egypt becomes one country ruled by a single king.
2686–2181 B.C.	The Old Kingdom period in ancient Egyptian history. The country's huge pyramids are built.
2055–1650 B.C.	The Middle Kingdom period in ancient Egyptian history. Trade increases with other nations in the region.
1550–1295 B.C.	The New Kingdom period in ancient Egyptian history. The country reaches new heights. It develops a strong army and large empire.
1490 B.C.	Queen Hatshepsut's reign begins.
1347 B.C.	King Tutankhamun's reign begins.
1290 B.C.	Ramses II's reign begins.
332 B.C.	Alexander the Great conquers Egypt.
323 B.C.	Alexander the Great dies of a fever.

51 B.C.	Cleopatra becomes queen of Egypt.
30 B.C.	Rome conquers Egypt. It becomes part of the Roman Empire until A.D. 639.
A.D. 1922	King Tutankhamun's tomb is discovered.

Dates given for ancient Egypt are not exact. Ancient Egyptian history reaches far back in time and differing dates are often found for the same event or period. These dates should be seen only as a general guide.

Glossary

architecture—The design of buildings.

artisan—A highly skilled craftsperson.

astronomy—The study of the stars and planets.

constellation—A group of stars.

dynasty—A line of rulers from the same family.

engineering—The design of various structures.

flax—A type of plant used to make linen.

herdsmen—People who tend a herd of animals.

hieroglyphic writing—A type of picture writing used in ancient Egypt.

irrigation—The use of canals or pipes to bring water to a dry area.

linen—Cloth.

livestock—Farm animals.

papyrus—A plant from which a type of paper was made in ancient Egypt.

pharaoh—An ancient Egyptian ruler.

For More Information

Bailey, Linda. *Adventures in Ancient Egypt*. Tonawanda, N.Y.: Kids Can Press, 2000.

Gibbons, Gail. *Mummies, Pyramids, and Pharaohs: A Book About Ancient Egypt*. Boston: Little Brown, 2003.

Graff, Jackie. *Tutankhamun: The Boy King*. New York: Peter Bendrick Books, 2002.

Holub, Joan. *Valley of the Golden Mummies*. New York: Grosset & Dunlap, 2002.

Honan, Linda. *Spend the Day in Ancient Egypt: Projects and Activities That Bring the Past to Life*. New York: John Wiley & Sons, 1999.

Tanaka, Shelley. *Secrets of the Mummies; Uncovering the Bodies of Ancient Egyptians*. New York: Hyperion, 1999.

Winters, Kay. *Voices of Ancient Egypt*. Washington D.C.: National Geographic, 2003.

Wroble, Lisa A. *Kids in Ancient Egypt*. New York: Rosen, 2003.

Internet Addresses

The British Museum—Ancient Egypt

Learn all about life in ancient Egypt through this interesting and colorful web site. Do not miss the great photos.

<http://www.ancientegypt.co.uk>

NOVA Online/Pyramids—The Inside Story

Visit this web site and wander through the chambers and passageways of the Great Pyramid.

<http://www.pbs.org/>

In the "Explore" drop-down list, select "History." Under "Topic Index" at the right, click on "Ancient World." Scroll down and click on "Pyramids: The Inside Story" at the left under the "Nova" heading.

PBS—Secrets of the Pharaohs

An interactive web site about ancient Egypt's past. It includes maps, timelines, and photos.

<http://www.pbs.org/>

In the "Explore" drop-down list, select "History." Under "Topic Index" at the right, click on "Ancient World." Scroll down and click on "Secrets of the Pharaohs" at the left.

Index